All Aboard The Numpty Bus

All Aboard
The Numpty Bus

Martin Wildman

AGRE

For Sue

First published in 2003
by AGRE BOOKS
Groom's Cottage, Nettlecombe
Bridport, Dorset, DT6 3SS

www.agrebooks.co.uk

Typeset by Agre Books, printed and bound by
Short Run Press, Exeter, Devon

ISBN 0-9538000-8-3

A CIP record for this book is available
from the British Library

CONTENTS

SLEEVES OUTSIDE MY COAT

Sleeves outside my coat!
Sleeves outside my coat!
Will someone shoot me in the head
or shall I cut my throat?
When different women serve my needs
the only thing they note
is that I've got my jumper sleeves
outside my bloody coat.

Did Churchill have this problem?
Did Larkin, when he wrote
'This was Mr Bleaney's room,'
have sleeves outside his coat?
Did Shakespeare show his shirt sleeves?
Did Marilyn in *Time*?
Did Holmes laugh at poor Watson's cuffs
as they solved another crime?

But who knows if our history
is shrouded in such mystery
because those ancient years
are marked by those who did the deeds?
Did Arthur in his majesty
conceal a bigger tragedy
because he went to Avalon
with dragging jumper sleeves?

Numpties

HERE we are aboard the Numpty Bus. You and me on an uphill and downhill ride with dubious brakes. This is a collection of my prose and poetry which should allow you to understand what it is like to be part of my disorganised mind. Let me first explain what it means to be a Numpty.

The word Numpty comes from Scottish slang and means somebody who is an idiot. Where I come from down in the fresh, distinctive land of Devonshire, it can also mean a yokel, or, more specifically, a village idiot or fool. Stereotypically, these people were thought of as having a gap in their teeth wide enough to drive a Morris Minor through, and a flat forehead from years of bashing it against a brick wall in the vain hope that sense will materialise. More recently, people have started to use the word Numpty as an insulting description of disabled people. I think it comes from the misconception that every person who is disabled is also somehow stupid. A Numpty Bus is one of those vehicles that is used to transport people like me from place to place. These vehicles are the only ones on the road that seem to be the mutant love child of a Land Rover and a fridge. But who cares?

I'm proud to be aboard the Numpty Bus, and I hope you are too.

Me

THIS is me. I am Martin Wildman; a man who is totally paralysed from the neck down. I am a 100 percent, bona-fide, 24-carat Numpty.

Of course, it wasn't always this way. I grew up in the village of Kingsteignton in South Devon, near to the market town of Newton Abbot. My Mum and Dad, June and Malc, brought me up with my two younger brothers, Steven and Ian. My Aunty Janet and Uncle Pete were always there to give us support, as were my maternal grandparents, Daisy and Bill. I attended the village infants, junior and comprehensive schools and left to study English, maths and economics A-Levels at Newton Abbot Sixth Form (Knowles Hill). I then left the Sixth Form to study at Plymouth Polytechnic. I had opportunity, happiness and good health but things were due to change.

On a particularly hot day in September 1990, me and a group of my friends decided to go to the beach. I have always loved the coast, swimming, surfing and relaxing, so we agreed to go to a place in the South Hams called Bantham. Unlike many areas on the south coast of Devon, it has good surf. Not only that, the whole atmosphere of Bantham, coupled with the view over the estuary towards Bigbury and Burgh Island, is inspiring. I can remember feeling that

This is me in 1979 aged 11, wearing my new school uniform and optional blazer. Mum was proud of how smart I looked in that blazer, but I wouldn't have worn it if I'd realised how many dead arms and grundies I was going to get. (A grundy is when other kids pull your underpants up your arse).

nothing could go wrong. Even though I had recently failed my accountancy degree (a subject which was never really up my street), I had an in-built peace and confidence that I have never had since. It was such a simple accident. I was mucking about in the estuary near the beach, I ran to the side of the water and dived in, hitting my head on the riverbed, which, although I didn't realise it at the time, caused me to break my neck. I was instantly paralysed and helpless, but I was calm and free of any pain. I floated off, face down, with the current like a human raft, and I remember thinking 'well, I'm going to die but it doesn't seem that bad.'

Some minutes later, my younger brother Steve pulled me out. I was in a hell of a state. I was useless, all floppy. Luckily, there was a doctor on the beach at the time. He gave me the kiss of life and I can remember him reassuring everybody saying that even though my breathing was shallow, I *was* breathing. My girlfriend Sue was distraught and bewildered; she was the only person in a worse state than me, except that her distress was mental.

Then, in a brief pocket of jumbled time, a helicopter arrived and airlifted me to Derriford Hospital, where I spent the next couple of weeks with less than professional nursing care. I should have been in traction for at least a month and a half, but the nurses had me sitting in an armchair within a week.

God knows what additional spinal damage was done, but I survived. Once I was relatively stable, I was transferred to the Duke of Cornwall Spinal Injuries Unit at Salisbury District Hospital (which was then still known as Odstock Hospital) where

I would have my so-called 'rehabilitation'. Being hospitalised long-term is different to anything else that most people experience during their lives. You are taken out of normality and thrust into a totally sterile artificial world. As a high level tetraplegic (or, as I would be called in the States, a quadriplegic), rehabilitation is not an adequate word to describe what happens to you in hospital. I came across phrases like 'long-term low quality life' and 'little chance of significant recovery.' You realise then that there is nothing that anyone can do. So, instead of spending a small amount of time getting better, I spent a whole year in hospital preparing for my life as a disabled person. I was 22.

Whenever I think about it, I start to get palpitations. As Japanese glam heavy metal band EZO. say, I have a 'flashback heart attack.' I suppose that I shouldn't think about the past too much. I should be living in the present and thinking of the future. Generally, I do this but occasionally I find myself wallowing, fantasising about how things could have been and how things might be now, even though I have a happy life with my partner Sue, living in a pretty bungalow in Kingsteignton with our two crazy cats, Ozzy and Minx, and our neurotic dog, Jadie.

So how do I feel now? Sometimes I hate myself. Sometimes I wish I would just give up and die.

Even now, I have tantalising recurring dreams about being cured and being better. They give me hope and false hope in equal quantities. Most of the time though, despite bouts of soul-crunching depression and spells of almost incomprehensible happiness, I think about what I can do and what I can achieve with my life. I suppose that as long as I keep active and remain relatively interesting then perhaps it won't be too bad.

Two things that I have learned through my experiences, though, are that you can never take anything for granted, and that you can never have enough disposable latex gloves.

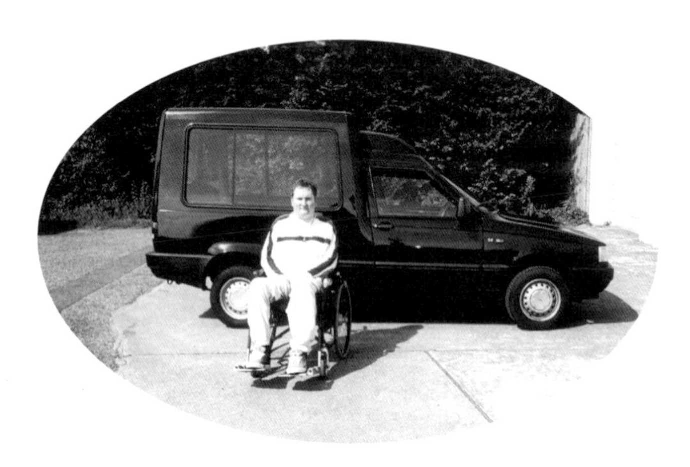

Me and my Numpty Bus at home in Kingsteignton

SOUTH AND WEST

'No need for you to cry, my lover,'
says Uncle's Cousin's maze half-brother.
'I am from the South and West!'
Tainted in the South and West.
Less than nothing.
Modern Greek.
Let me drink my cider.

Accent is a crutch to bear.
Blackened teeth,
Unruly hair.
'I am from the South and West!'
Never left the South and West.
Just above
Your average sheep.
Salad is for wimps.

Not a Geordie.
Not a Scot.
Am I happy with what I've got?
'I am from the South and West!'
Broken in the South and West.
Driving tractors,
Eating hay,
Crisps and fags for tea.

Coughing gently,
Looking down,
Apathy falls all around.
'I am from the South and West!'
Born into the South and West.
Clotted mind,
Pasty face,
Honey-covered words.

The West Country

I REALLY love the West Country. In an ideal world, everybody would live here (which would, of course, spoil it). There is something very special about the place. People that live elsewhere are often hooked once they experience it and come back again and again. However, non-West Country people (even those who enjoy the area) tend to view us locals in a derogatory way. To people who live in the North, West Country people are the thickest of the southerners. To people of the South, (I mean, people who live to the East of Dorset), West Country people are yokels who couldn't be intelligent if they wanted to be. People who live here feel somehow detached from the rest of the UK. We are not Northerners, we are not Southerners, we are West Country people and we are proud of it.

A recent survey of 'sexy' accents of Britain showed that a West Country accent was the second least desirable in the country. Only a Birmingham accent was less desirable. The unfashionable nature of the West Country accent is borne out by its absence on TV. When I switch on my television set, I only hear other, funkier accents. Even Birmingham is heard more often on television than West Country. There are no major celebrities with West Country accents. Sure, some people on local television have West Country accents, but, then again, they are bound to be, aren't they? And OK, you could include, I suppose, Jethro and the Wurzels, but do you think that they really count? Look at the people who are on the latest cool children's programmes and the latest music programmes. Can you hear any one there who speaks with a thick West Country accent? No. Neither can I.

All things aside though, coming from this part of the world does have its advantages. It has got to be one of the most beautiful places in the country. Its beauty constantly amazes me. Even though Kingsteignton is not the most beautiful village in the world, there is easy access to the sea, the moorland, to farmland, forests, estuaries and, well too many things to list here. So, I don't really care if you live in London, Liverpool, Newcastle, or any of these places which are deemed cool when you can't breathe in the beauty of your home just by travelling a few miles, the way that I can.

I feel linked to this area. As far as Kingsteignton goes, my family tree reaches back over 300 years. There are times when I think I would like to live somewhere else, like Scotland or Wales, but I always seem to be drawn back to here. Sometimes I think that it just wouldn't seem right to live anywhere else because in my heart I'm just a simple West Country boy.

The Bickham Blood

KINGSTEIGNTON is an ancient village which was founded by the Anglo-Saxons over 1,000 years ago. There must have been people living in Kingsteignton from at least the Iron Age onwards because Iron Age workings have been found nearby. Kingsteignton is mentioned in the *Anglo-Saxon Chronicle* where it is recorded as Tegntun. This means 'farm on the River Teign'; the 'Kings' part refers to the fact that it was situated in the middle of a Crown Estate. Kingsteignton was probably a very important settlement in Saxon times. In around the year 1000 AD, the village was attacked by those angry, hairy Hell's Angels of the Dark Ages, the Vikings. In the early 20th century a Viking longship was dug up at one of the local clay works, although more recent research proved that it was in fact an old canal barge. In the Domesday Book, Kingsteignton was still a royal estate, and during the reign of King Henry II, Richard De Bourdon, became the first Lord of the Manor of Kingsteignton. One of the most important events in the village's history happened in the 13th century, when monks from Salisbury built a channel to divert water from marshes situated between Rydon and Oakford and created a brook which still runs through the village today. To be a true Kingsteigntonian, it is said that you should have fallen into the brook and I think most children that have grown up here have done so many times.

The famous Kingsteignton Ram Roasting Fair is related to the creation of the leat. Legend says during an extremely severe drought, the brook dried-up denying the village its main source of water. A local wise woman suggested that they should sacrifice a ram in the streambed. The villagers agreed wholeheartedly with this suggestion and rounded up the nearest ram. As soon as they had cut the unfortunate animal's throat, the brook flowed again and this probably postponed the wise woman's death due to a severe case of being burnt at the stake. Each year a fair is held to remember this sacrifice and a ram is killed and fed to the locals. In late Victorian times, the Ram was decorated and paraded through the villages of Bishopsteignton, Ideford and Kingsteignton. The festivities were held at what is now Crossley Moor Road, where the leat still runs. Villagers are known as Ramroasters for obvious reasons, and the fair is still held every May Bank Holiday, with huge amounts of extremely greasy ram sandwiches and rolls being served to an unsuspecting public.

My family has a special connection with Kingsteignton going back years through generations of Harrises and Bickhams. My grandfather on the Harris side was William Harris; he was married to my Nan, Daisy. Everybody knew him as Bill, and he was a clay worker for most of his life, working for the local clay firm WBB. Clay gave a lot of jobs to local families. During the war, Gramp was a motor torpedo boat gunner and it obviously had a massive effect on his thinking. In fact, Gramp really never left the war because he relived it day after day by recounting the stories to his family. He tended to pick on his completely uninterested grandchildren. Yawning or laughing were frowned upon as Gramp went over and over and over stories of cowardly Nazis, cowardly Yanks and braver than brave British Tommies who would always come out on top in the end. Gramp died relatively young at the age of 64, because earlier in his life he had been a very heavy smoker. Even though at times he could often bore the legs off an oak table, we all still miss him terribly. My cousin Kate, who was only a toddler when he died, would play his Country and Western music tapes constantly just to remind herself of him.

Gramp's father was Fred Harris. He was my great-grandfather and was an imposing figure. My memory of him is sketchy because he died when I was 10. He was a giant-sized man, over 6ft tall and broad as a bus, who worked hard all of his life. He was a Navy man as well. He married my great grandmother Selina Harris, whose maiden name was Hewings. I can remember her well

Great Grampy Fred Harris working in the local quarry. He was a big man, but it's unknown whether the barrow shown here contains an average load, or whether he overfilled it for the purpose of posing for a picture.

because she died when I was 19. She was, in contrast, a tiny woman who shrunk as she got older. She was very caring and could be strict as her five sons found out on many occasions. The last time I saw her she was in a nursing home and it was winter. I had come to see her and she wanted to hold my hands. I remember her saying 'your hands are so cold, so cold.' It made me want to take her home with me, even though I was still a teenager. She lived until she was 100.

My mother's cousin, Richard Harris, has researched our family tree tracing back the Harris line. Fred's father was James Harris and his wife was Ellen Bickham. From there the Bickham line goes back approximately 300 years, all of the members of the family tree coming from Kingsteignton itself. Ellen's father was William, whose father was William, whose father was Thomas, whose father was Thomas. This last Thomas married a Mary Martin in Kingsteignton. Then the Bickham line dries up in the late 18th century, however we do know that Bickhams were still living in the village in the 17th century.

I feel like I have a strong tie to Kingsteignton. It could be the Bickham blood in me or it might be something else. It is amazing to imagine that inheritance has been passed down from generation to generation all growing up in Kingsteignton. It makes you think about reincarnation and souls being recycled over and over again. The Bickhams must have had very different lives to what we have now, but they *were* alive. I used to lie awake at night thinking about how it seems like our time, or fate, is already mapped out; somehow already decided, like the present is already old. Almost as if the Bickhams, the Harrises, all families are destined to live their lives again through later generations.

Once, I was flicking through some of the old photographs in one of the books about Kingsteignton that Richard has written when I came across an image of my great Nan's brother George Hewings. I could not believe what I was seeing. George would have been my great-great-uncle. In the picture, he is holding a massive shire horse in all its regalia. But, if you look closely enough, he looks almost exactly like my brother Ian when he was aged 16. Spookily enough, George was probably aged about 16 when that picture was taken. It's the eyes I think, it's all in the eyes. George looks at me from years ago, trying to tell me something. I think he is trying to say that I should never forget where I come from. Perhaps, we are all recycled. Perhaps, the reason that George looks like my brother Ian is the souls of our ancestors are reused and recycled over and over again. The problem with having a strong tie to Kingsteignton is that you realise you are linked more to the past of the village than the present.

Great-great Uncle George Hewings with a shire horse dressed in regalia for the Ram Roast Fair. Despite his old-fashioned clothes, George looks exactly like my brother Ian did as a teenager. He even has Ian's cheesed-off teenage expression.

This is more obvious today than it was in years gone by. Kingsteignton still has picturesque parts. St Michael's Church is gorgeous. It has a wonderful churchyard and areas around it like Sandpath Road (where many old buildings remain), Berry Lane (where the old brook runs), and Golvers Hill (which has some old thatched buildings) are still very beautiful but these areas are in the minority. Today, Kingsteignton is an ugly, sprawling place. There is far too much new housing which has eaten away the green areas that used to break up the buildings. Areas which were unspoilt when I was a child, such as Rydon, which was a mass of green fields and woodland, are overflowing with cardboard box houses that look like tombstones to me. Kingsteignton is full of commuters because of its easy access to other bigger towns. These commuters always seem to be *leaving* the village. Even the Ram Roast, which is nowadays held at a local field called Oakford Lawn, is under threat. There has recently been a big kerfuffle about the fact that planners want to build houses on the lawn. Hopefully, this will never happen but the fact that it is even being considered shows how things have changed over the years. Today, Kingsteignton is a place where kids hang around on street corners destroying trees and kicking Coke cans into vandalised walls and drinking cheap cider. As much as I love the place, I can't help but think that the community spirit sometimes seems to be waning.

When it's good though, Kingsteignton's community spirit shines through and refuses to die. Through village activities like football, skittles, darts and other pastimes, the people are fighting to maintain the independence, self-reliance and character of the area. Places like the pubs, British Legion, bowls clubs and football clubs are where old Kingsteignton families can gather and reminisce. Only through supporting our rural areas and people can we preserve the significance of the West Country. A sense of community and

One of the butchers employed by Ned Willis, slicing up the Ram Roast. Butchering the Ram is a great honour.

belonging is not found in bricks and mortar, clubs and establishments; it resides in the hearts of all of us. No matter how big and chaotic Kingsteignton gets, the real Kingsteignton is inside the local people. That's what the Bickhams thought and that's what I think.

I believe the Kingsteignton that resides in my heart is more real than the actual place. One day, I may leave in search of hedgerows, fields, woodland, the mountains, silence, but, if that ever happens, I will take the essence of the old village with me.

The Easy Life

WHEN you are disabled like me, it is interesting to see how able-bodied people view you. I'm not talking about bigotry or some type of discrimination, I'm talking about how able-bodied people think they would react if they were disabled. I get, on the whole, a lot of sympathy and pity for the situation that I am in. People imagine that to be paralysed like I am would be the worst thing in the world. Well, it's probably news to people that it isn't. Life for me isn't hell. Life for me is tiresome and *mentally* exhausting.

It's the general difficulties of living that really get me down. Imagine, if you can, that almost every action you do throughout the day is hard to accomplish. Getting out of bed, washing, cleaning your teeth, having a shave, even dressing is difficult. As well as being hard, the actions are not being performed *by* me, they are being performed *on* me by another person (usually a carer). This makes everything seem more drawn-out and mentally tedious. Imagine, for example, having a shower. Firstly, because you can't do it yourself, you have to ask somebody else to do it for you, which is embarrassing and degrading. Once you've gotten over that, you realise how drawn out and exhausting it can be. First, I transfer from my bed to a shower chair with the use of an electric hoist and sling; the carer puts the sling under me while I am on the bed. The shower chair is cumbersome and uncomfortable, so five minutes are spent positioning me in the chair so that I don't swan dive on to the floor.

Then I am pushed into the shower room. The shower is switched on and my carer sets about washing me from head to foot. Showers were not designed to be used on a person sitting on a chair so doing a good job is difficult. Then my hair is washed – I am used to holding my breath whilst this is happening (a knack for someone with a diminished lung capacity). I am rinsed and then I am towel dried, before my hair is blow dried in front of the mirror. Then back by the bed and the sling is put under me again. I am hoisted on to the bed and the sling is removed. I am dried again then I am dressed in a quarter of an hour stint which resembles Hulk Hogan wrestling with Rowan Atkinson. Then sling under, hoist, and I'm in my wheelchair; an hour of struggling and ready for the rest of the morning's routine.

Easy tasks for me can be difficult and time-consuming. My love of books, and more specifically reading anything (whether it's reading a novel, the newspaper, a comic book, or any poetry), has given me a real problem. My carers have to turn the pages (which disrupts my thought processes) and I have to read using a beanbag tray, a wooden plinth and a sheet of Perspex to keep the pages down. It can be a real pain and I would read a lot more if the procedure were easier. Even writing this book has been a laborious task at times because instead of simply typing in the words with a keyboard, I have to use a voice recognition headset for the bulk of the text (which takes practice, patience and the vocal dexterity of a horse-racing commentator with rubber lips) and a headset-mouse for the corrections (with which I can only type in one letter per mouse click. It's very slow). My love of reading and writing seems like a relationship with a woman who's good in bed but an Exeter City fan; difficult but rewarding in the end.

When I am outside the house, say, for example, being pushed around town, life is complicated and arduous. Everything in the modern world of the town centre seems to be made specifically for making my life hard. Steps, sticky doors, cobbles, coconut mats, narrow aisles, boxes, potholes and many, many other obstacles get in my way. People are my main problem, though. Many of them must have some type of sheep in their ancestry (well, this is Devon!) They hang around in an extended pack, milling about, getting in my way. They stop walking abruptly, causing my pusher to stop dead, making me practically shoot out of my wheelchair (thank God for seat belts!). I actually chuckle to myself when I run over somebody's foot; it gives me a type of sadistic pleasure knowing that for a split-second somebody has experienced the pain of a dodgy wheelchair manoeuvre.

When I'm in town, I like to look for new and old books. If I park in front of a bookcase full of books that I want to look at, then another difficulty arises. This is the type of speech that I come out with when trying to get my carer to pick out a book that I want to look at:

'Right. See that orange book. No not that one. Point if you can. Up three shelves. No, up three. To the left slightly. Now, see that book by T.S. Eliot. No, T.S. Eliot, not R.S. Thomas. The orange one. Go left five books. Another one. And another. Now see the green book. Not that one, the one next to it. Now go left until you get to the orange book. Yes that one. Now get me the one directly to the left of it. The other left. OK. Now pick it up and open it to the inside front cover. Turn the page over. No, the other way. Turn over again. And again. And again. OK I'll read that.'

And all just to read the contents page of a poetry book that anyone else could pick up in two seconds flat!

My life can be tedious, problematic and tiresome. Sometimes, just sitting in my wheelchair and doing nothing gets me down. Imagine if you can having to sit in front of the TV, hour after hour, not doing a single thing. Every other evening, sitting there, I play a kind of solitaire musical statues, getting bored out of my tiny mind. When other people, I mean able-bodied people, sit watching the TV, they do things. They scratch their heads, they pick their teeth, pat the dog, change the channels, glance at a magazine, lie outstretched on the settee and so on. Sitting down and doing nothing is so mind numbingly tiresome that sometimes I think that my brain has been paralysed as well. Thank God that it hasn't.

When I think about how tedious my life can be, it makes me realise that it is not all down to my disability. I think that it is a modern problem. Many of us find that our day-to-day lives are not fulfilling and rewarding. Thinking back over the years, I can remember when, even before my accident, I became disillusioned and thought of my life as insignificant. How many of us have thought of quitting our jobs as solicitors, accountants, tax inspectors, business managers and so on to become crofters and self-sufficient goatherds. To give up everything for a rewarding and satisfying way of life.

Many of us have dreamt of it but I have experienced it first hand when I used to visit my great grandfather and grandmother. I knew them as Nanny and Grampy Yeo. Their actual names wereFrank Yeo and Lillian Yeo. They were wonderful lovely people who lived at Ingsdon,

LEFT: Grampy Yeo wearing his Army clobber by a patch of his famous cabbages. Churchill felt that Gramp's skills could be best employed in WWII fighting the Nazis in the Orkney Isles. Gramp was more likely to invite a German in for meat patties and cider than bayonet him.

RIGHT: Nan and Grampy in their orchard.

Devon, on the Bickington Road. They lived in an old converted mill house which was called, as you might imagine, Mill House. It sits in the gorgeous River Lemon valley, and is surrounded by beautiful woodland and farmland.

Grampy Yeo was a 'good old boy' and a marvellous grandfather. He was always happy, always full of fun, and he had an impish look in his eye. Nanny Yeo was a wonderfully caring woman, who worked hard and knew how to enjoy life. They were a pleasure to be with. They loved the countryside with a passion and taught us about the glories of nature. Gramp revelled in his gardening (they never went hungry for vegetables when Gramp was around). I can remember the flocks of chickens strutting around the adjoining fields. The chickens provided eggs and one of my earliest memories is of plunging my hand under a disgruntled chicken and trying to grasp a fresh warm egg. Nanny Yeo was well know for providing the biggest roast meals ever. She would get upset when her great grandchildren wouldn't eat all of their meal, even though there was enough food on each plate to keep a Ukrainian powerlifter happy for the whole day. A standard meal for a ten-year-old would be two pork chops, four roast potatoes, cabbage, a Yorkshire pudding, runner beans, broadbeans and gravy. Of course, then came the pudding; some type of hot tart or pie with rivers of custard. Those days when I used to go out to Ingsdon were very happy. I can always remember sunshine, children laughing and a general atmosphere of love and happiness in the air. Looking back on those times, I realise that they were very important to me. It was a time when I was contented with my life. Today I realise that what makes me happy is different. My life can seem tedious and occasionally painfully meaningless. It can make me very unhappy. I do go through periods of terrible depression and my relationship with Sue is often strained close to breaking point. We have to put up with difficulties that most people don't have. My Nan and Grampy Yeo were happy with their lives of hard graft, mental relaxation and simplicity. It was how they wanted to live.

When I failed my business degree, it made me look long and hard at what I wanted out of life. I decided that I would do something which was beneficial to mankind and that I would enjoy. If I would have had the choice I would have chosen to be a Dartmoor Ranger, somebody who works with animals, a charity worker or even a firefighter. I have also always had an ambition to own and work in a coffee bar and bookshop; that would have been wonderful. These ambitions that I oncehad grate at me, making me realise that I am deeply unhappy with how things have turned out.

What you see before you is not who I am. Deep down I'm not a disabled man. I am somebody who loves to walk in the wilderness, somebody who loves to compete in sport of all types, somebody who loves to swim, throw sticks for the dog and even likes to climb the Tors of Dartmoor. When you boil it all down, I believe my occasional disillusionment with my life is because I did not choose to be the way I am. I did not choose to spend by life in a wheelchair. Choice is a basic human need and I have been denied that at a fundamental level. All of the things that make me happy in the short term, like watching Torquay United, going on outings and even my success as a writer, I would give up to be able-bodied again. Not because I am ashamed of being disabled, but because deep down to be me is to be able-bodied. I am more a crofter at heart than a writer; if I were really who I wanted to be, this book would have never been written. Because of this, I sometimes wish it never was.

STUMPS

It was hot.
It was very hot.
Hot as a picnic on Mercury.
Dry as a mouthful of sand.

When the brussel sprouts
were picked, plump and juicy,
we worked the graveyard of stumps
in the sweltering heat.
For young boys
this was identity.
We were no longer annoyances
to be kicked out from beneath
old leather shoes.
This task needed no training.
No experience.
We were as good as the next man.

We were contenders,
the stumps were the champions.
Rough and yellowing,
hard and upright.
Infertile old men,
stubborn as a tree.

We gripped them fast,
as if surprise would shock them
from their thirsty beds.
Then we pulled,
blew steam like a engine.
Clods flew,
a mud cloudburst.

Once the stumps were gone,
we could quench our dry mouths
in illegality, with brown ale.

But there was always one stump,
a giant, a king,
that could resist a young boy's arms.
So Grampy Yeo would show us
how boys are not men,
One-handed.

Grampy Yeo outside a pub. All his mates knew him as Chappy Yeo. His local was The Welcome Stranger near Bickington where he played euchre, a popular card game, which he loved. He won many matches using his 'blind' eye to glance into his opponent's hand.

Married to Torquay United

WHEN I broke my neck and realised that I couldn't do many things that I had taken for granted before, I was distraught, gutted, sick to the core and I thought that life wasn't worth living. One of the reasons was that I could no longer play football, and, as many people know, there is no substitute for that.

Eventually, I thought about the possibility of supporting my local football league team with a little more vigour than I had before. That team was, and is, Torquay United.

When I was a child, I always supported Manchester United. That's from about 1973 through until 1989. They did win some things, but not a great deal. My favourite player was the dashing right winger Steve Coppell and as a lad, I always wanted to emulate him. Torquay were really my second team; I always checked their result on a Saturday and was happy when they won but it was a minor concern.

After 1990, when my connection to football through playing was severed, I decided to re-establish the link by watching football in a more serious way by supporting Torquay. This was because they played close by and it seemed like it could be fun. At that time, I did not realise how strong my feelings for the club would become. I am pretty much Torquay United mad. I go to see every home league match and some away matches, and, since 1990, I have seen some great highs and some horrible, depressing lows.

My favourite player is Rodney Jack; a fantastically skilful striker who was a joy to watch. I have seen many players come to wear the yellow of Torquay over the years. I have seen our chairman change Torquay from a team that was heavily in debt to a team with no debts. I just keep hoping that one day we get the success that I think that we deserve.

Seeing Torquay United play, week in week out, makes you realise that football isn't football unless it means something. When you have seen the crushing, gut-churning, amateurish performances that I have seen over the years, it makes you realise what success is like. Also, at a live match, you see things that you wouldn't normally see on TV. I have seen St John Ambulance men fall over in six inches of mud, fights between rival fans (especially Torquay and Exeter fans), people who strip down practically naked and then do the conga, and people who dress up as large furry animals. I have also had people spit at me and verbally abuse me at matches. Yes, to some people, football is more important than life and death... People who are not normally bigots will use my status as a disabled person to hurt me, just because their team is losing. I have been called a spastic a few times in my life, nearly every time it was at a football match. Even officials, coaches, physios and managers have stood directly in front of me so I can't see the game (mentioning no names - Peter Shreeves!). This is because they believe their job is *so* important that preventing one spectator from seeing the match is justified. Funnily enough, this last point shows how some people who are 'inside' football treat us civilians, no matter who you are. 'Oh, you're a man in a wheelchair with an obscured view, well hard luck!' To be frank, these people would stand in front of Jesus, the Pope and the Dalai Lama if they were watching a match. These negative events have been on the decline over the last decade though.

Some unusual things occur at Torquay matches. One memorable event was when a naked man ran onto the pitch, after his team, Blackpool, had taken a 2-nil lead (obviously celebrating madly), only for him to see Torquay pull one goal back (to make it 2-1), and then for him to see Torquay score twice in the last two minutes of injury time so that Torquay won 3 goals to 2; injury time which would not have been added on if this guy had not stripped off and run on the pitch in the first place! I have also seen a man invade the pitch dressed in a kilt and a bin-liner, wearing a mask of ex-Boyzone singer Ronan Keating, and a man who

Me and my brother Steve sometime around 1995, ready for Kingsteignton Athletic's Herald Cup Final match, which Kingsteignton lost. Dressing up as a clown for Torquay is quite unnecessary, there's often too much comedy already.

was convinced that ex-Torquay and ex-Crewe player Stuart Evans was God. Torquay United matches have a homely feel. I often eat cakes which have been made for me by one of the player's Nan and her friend (guess who Ryan Ashington! Hello, Joyce and Megs!) We often eat excellent rock and fairy cakes made for all the Torquay United wheelchair fans (that's me and my mate Paul); I think they worry that we might need a sugar boost at these matches from time to time (how true!)

I am still surprised by what supporting a lower league football team can do to me. When Torquay actually *win* something, I get emotionally moved. When we won the last play-off semi-final, I almost cried. All that frustration at losing again and again, made me realise that I genuinely care about this bloody stupid old team more than I think I do. It made me realise that if I didn't care, there would be no point in going.

So why do I go to see Torquay play every week? What does seeing Torquay play do for me that nothing else can? Well, I think that supporting a football team gives you a sense of belonging. I believe it taps an ancient tribal instinct. It gives people a release for their pent-up energy and makes them believe that they are not alone. The actual match is a type of combat between rival clans, and I think it gives people the type of feeling that only conflict and war can give. In ancient times, men would congregate around the camp-fire and talk of glory in battle, and now, men meet in pubs and talk about how Stockport hammered Grimsby. I suppose, when you reduce it down to that, it sounds a little bit sad.

Also, I think there is something about supporting a team which doesn't achieve much. I believe that many of us find it hard not to support the underdog. I once watched England play Albania, and found myself unwittingly cheering for Albania. Funnily enough, my brother Steve (who is also a Torquay fan) was doing the same. In biblical times, we would have been in the David fan club as opposed to the Goliath supporters.

On the radio the other day they had a football expert talking about supporting your favourite football team. He said that he believed it was extremely regrettable that most men regarded supporting their football team as more important than marriage. The interviewer protested that this was a load of rubbish, so the expert replied that about 50 per cent of marriages end in divorce and most football fans (he said about 90 per cent) never change their football team.

Men show more loyalty to their football team than to their wives. After all how many Liverpool fans do you think secretly have football affairs with Manchester United? Next to none.

So what does going to see Torquay mean to me? All that I know is that without football, the universe would be a little bit less interesting and I would have nowhere to go on a Saturday afternoon.

JUST A SPOONFUL

A woman from Surrey,
filled with herself,
once said that etiquette
provided a full set of rules
for life.

You know what she means.
It's vital to know when to use
the fork
or the knife,
the heroin
or the chocolate.

Like hell it is.

Perhaps if she'd concentrated life
down to the thick green liquid
that is mine,
there just isn't any other way
to eat
spaghetti
or stew,
curry
or custard;
maybe then
she might do what I do
and use the spoon
for everything.

Newton Abbot

I HAVE spent a lot of time in Newton Abbot, socialising, buying things and generally trying to have a good time.

Newton Abbot was a settlement in prehistoric times. There is an Iron Age fort behind Bradley Manor and Roman roads close by. At the time of the Norman Conquest, a castle stood in the Highweek area. A family going by the name of Bushel inherited the settlement and the Newton Abbot area originally developed from two manors within their borders. These were Newton Abbot and Newton Bushel. The smaller Manor of Newton Bushel was invited to form a united council in 1901 (eventually, the name Newton Bushel fell out of use and that area is now known as Highweek). In 1846, the railway arrived and Newton Abbot became famous for having one of the earliest railway stations.

Newton Abbot has always been a market town. For decades Newton (as many of the locals know it) has had a market on Wednesday afternoon. It was originally mainly for farmers, who brought all their cattle, sheep, pigs and other livestock for sale. Because of its popularity, market stalls selling all manner of products sprang up. My older relatives say that years ago the market was quite an event and very popular. It ran down the major streets of the town and the sights and smells must have been spectacular. By all accounts, Newton was absolutely gorgeous in those days. With the River Lemon running right through the middle of the town, it was one of the prize towns of Devon. Things have changed a little since then.

Today, Newton is slightly run-down. It has terrible traffic problems. Everybody passes through Newton and nobody stops there. Some of the buildings look very industrial, even though Newton is supposed to be a tourist spot. Although it always seems to be busy in the town centre, tourism is failing the town. It isn't able to pull in the numbers that it used to, and, for anybody that knows the town well, the reason is obvious. Many towns and villages have features which are appealing; they may be pretty, they may have a range of attractions, they may have shops which are quirky and unusual, but Newton doesn't have any of these qualities any more. I blame the planners myself. Newton has been allowed to become cancerous and uninviting.

However, for some reason, I still like the place. If you know where to look, it still has nice qualities. Compared to Kingsteignton, there are a lot of green areas. William of Orange declared himself King of England at the clock tower and there is still a monument there to mark the event. It has good pubs and some good cafes. Even though the market is not what it used to be, it is still worth a visit.

Growing up nearby, Newton was the place I liked to spend my pocket money and I'll always be partial to it. Being a seventies' child, the 50p that I got each week was very important to me. They were shiny, unusually shaped and as exciting as a doubloon. 50p could buy quite a lot in those days. When you are six or seven, you don't want to spend your new wealth on useful items, you want spend it on sweets and poor-quality, lower end of the market novelties. You want to buy rubber snakes, plastic beetles, itching powder, jumping frogs and fake tattoos. I get a sort of tingle when I remember what it was like to spend money in those days. Parting with money today just doesn't seem the same.

Well, that's Newton Abbot for you. I sort of like it. It's one of those places that you think you hate but really, deep down, you have an affinity for. It's like your grandmother's flock wallpaper; on the surface, it's gaudy and offensive, but the sight of it stirs affectionate memories. Or perhaps not. One set of memories concerns the infamous East Street Shuffle. Best to deal with that in a separate chapter.

The East Street Shuffle

KINGSTEIGNTON is not on many people's list of hot spots to visit. You could, let's say, have a day out in Newton Abbot or Exeter, but if you said you were going for a day out in Kingsteignton, people might think you were a little mad. This is because the local attractions (like the swimming pool and shops) are mediocre and, lacking a village centre, it struggles to find an identity. Kingsteignton does have one thing going for it though - its pubs.

Some of the pubs are prominently advertised on road signs on the way into the village. Kingsteignton has, at last count, seven proper pubs. They are: *The Ten Tors* (a loud pub popular with tourists), *The Old Rydon* (a posh pub with good food), *The Sandygate* (a proper locals' pub with gargantuan food portions), *The King's Arms* (a rough pub with comprehensive football coverage), *The Passage House* (a definite food pub with excellent views of the local wildfowl) and my two locals: *The Bell* (a good standard pub with occasional unwanted karaoke) and *The Dewdrop* (a great locals' pub with an unrivalled Friday night meat draw). Drinking is definitely a family affair in Kingsteignton. In the evening there is nothing else to do, so, from father to son, alcohol is tradition. Here is where you live, here is where

The front of The Bell Inn *as it was in about 1920. Externally, it has changed little, but the interior is much more open plan. You can see the actual bell over the front door - nowadays it is kept inside.* The Bell's *best points are good value food and the occasional dodgy part-time rock guitarist.*

you work, here is where you drink. When you start drinking as a teenager, you realise why adults hang about in pubs so much. Yes, alcohol is great. It's not cheap, but who cares when it makes you fall over? It makes you attractive to the opposite sex (so you think at the time) and makes the opposite sex attractive to you. It gives you an incredible vocal speed, if not accuracy, and it turns everybody into 'my best mate'.

As you get older, priorities change. When you're young and you first start drinking, you brag to

Outside Ye Olde Cider Bar *in East Street, Newton Abbot, in the early 1900s. I hope that all those people have not just drunk a lot of cider. Even in those days, men who drank too much cider would have had to run to the toilet shouting 'Christ!' Picture reproduced courtesy of Newton Abbot Museum.*

your mates about how much you can drink, how much it costs you to get drunk and how great it is. When you're over 30, you brag to your mates about how little you can drink, how cheap you are to get drunk and how great it is. When you're extremely old, I suppose you are just grateful to be able to walk to the pub!

Drinking is really a young person's sport. When I was a teenager, Kingsteignton was not the place to drink if you wanted to be seen as trendy. The big smoke was Newton Abbot. That was a place of drinking legend, the place to be noticed, the place to be cool. I used to hang about in a group who was into Heavy Metal and the landlords of the public houses in Newton Abbot thought that we were trouble. One particular pub, *The Courtenay*, banned us from entering on numerous occasions. The excuses for doing this ranged from the tenuous to the ludicrous. Firstly, we were banned for 'wearing leather jackets'. Then, we were banned for 'singing too loudly'. Other excuses were used over the years, but none so bizarre as 'buying an illegal drink'.

(This last reason was justified though and my fault. Mind you, the landlord should have realised what I was doing. I mean, I did order half of Guinness in a pint glass plus eight different notorious shorts, but at least we shared it!)

As far as Newton Abbot goes, there is one street which has gone down in modern legend; East Street. It is a basic, rustic-looking street with seven of pubs in it. These are: *The Union*, *The White Hart*, *The Jolly Abbot*, *The Locomotive*, *The Dartmouth*, *Strikers Bar* (formerly *The Devon Arms*), and last of all, *Ye Olde Cider Bar*. The challenge was to visit each of these pubs in turn, drink, and survive. The real challenge was to manage a pint in each, finishing up with the dreaded cider in the last one. Accomplishing this feat was known as the East Street Shuffle. It was, and still is, the ultimate test for alcoholics, binge-drinkers and semi-professional tramps. People may well think that the trials of Hercules were tough, but, let's face it, Hercules never visited East Street.

From trying The East Street Shuffle, you learn one important lesson; drinking cider is a stupid think to do. Oh yes, if the Devil drinks alcohol (and I'm sure he does), he must drink cider. Also, it's possible that *Ye Olde Cider Bar* is just a colourful disguise for the gates of Hell. As you enter, a wave of smoke and vinegar assaults your senses. Your eyeballs water like you've bitten into a sour pickled onion. Your throat gags and your stomach groans in anticipation. The ancient walls are peeling with alcohol fume abuse. You look around for a sane person to rescue you, but there is no-one. So, you ask for a pint of cider. The landlord pours it out. This thick and viscous fluid is as cloudy as chicken soup, and you know that it is going to be nasty. As you drink, you begin to think that this was not a good idea. Your fading consciousness figures out that you're not going to be able to remember anything more of this night. Your brain packs up and leaves. Whether you're going to spend the rest of the night in some converted back cave in Satan's den having your nipples tweaked by unruly imps, or whether you'll spend it stumbling like a rag doll back home is anybody's guess, because you'll never be able to recall what happened...

Nowadays, I don't drink much alcohol. This is a great shame, because I really used to enjoy it. I have a little thing called dehydration to deal with, and I cannot afford to be dehydrated, because it can lead to urine infections, bladder blockages and possibly a condition called autonomic dysreflexia. This is when my bladder inflates too much and, normally because of a urinary blockage, cannot empty itself. This can be unpleasant and even life threatening since my blood pressure increases rapidly to head-popping proportions. I feel ill when I'm dehydrated because of body signals which I get with an uncomfortable bladder, and also I think I get some psychosomatic warnings as well due to my fear of dysreflexia.

Sometimes, I think that it isn't really too bad that I can't drink alcohol. I know that beer tasted great when I was young and somehow it doesn't taste as good now. Anyway, even when I was young, I never could manage the East Street Shuffle and I doubt now that I ever will.

THE DEMON

He seems quite benign,
No threat
You think.
Only a few inches high,
An innocent
As clear as an evangelist's thought.
Blond bubbles
Burst open on his head.
There seems to be
A halo of apple in the air,
But perhaps not.
He is a friend
To be savoured.
He is sourly sweet.

But when you're lying on your gentle bed
And the room spins like a whirligig,
And your guts feel totally toxic
And your brain shrivels down
To the size of a raisin;
When your eyeballs
Are as dry as sloes,
You will regret
Entertaining
Cider.

Harry O

BETWEEN Newton Abbot and Bickington is a lovely stretch of deciduous woodland called Bradley Woods. It is just off a place called Baker's Park, which is generally used by dog-walkers and amateur footballers (brings a whole new meaning to 'dirty players'). It is a really nice area and probably one of the best open spaces in Newton Abbot. When I was 14, my cousin Scott told me that Bradley Woods had an unusual inhabitant, known as Harry O.

Harry O was said to be tramp who lived near some limekilns and spent his time chasing young girls and scaring old people. As a young lad, this seemed pretty real and I can remember being quite wary of walking through those woods, especially if I was on my own. My brothers, Scott, his brother David and me often used to play in the River Lemon and I can still hear them saying 'I wonder if Harry O is watching us,' and 'watch out, Harry O's going to get you.'

I always imagined that Harry O was a strange mish-mash of a creature; part human, part tramp and part Yeti. Harry O was a frightening apparition. I could almost see him shuffling around those limekilns, returning to his wet cave at night, eating fungi and picking the twigs out of his spindly beard. Harry O was a poor man's

Bigfoot. I could never imagine an SAS-type naturalist hunting him with a hypodermic needle gun, hoping to get a DNA sample from his backside (like you see on some nature programmes), because Harry was a third-rate monster. Yes, Harry O was to monster mythology what Kajagoogoo singer Limahl was to pop music.

It wasn't until later that I discovered that there was a better known Harry O. At the time, I almost did not believe it. Another Harry O? Surely not. But there was. He was the star of a mid-seventies detective series which was called (oh yes) Harry O. The series wasn't shown much in Britain, apart from late night on ITV, but, at its peak, it did have quite a good following in the USA. Harry O was played by David Janssen. He was an unconventional private investigator, who lived in a beachfront cottage near San Diego, California, and he was known for always using public transport rather than his car, which was always breaking down. He was an ex-Marine and ex-cop who was pensioned off after being injured in the line of duty, and, seeing that the pension was inadequate, he supplemented his income by taking cases that interested him. He was always having run-ins with the police for his unusual methods and this caused him to move his agency to Santa Monica. Helping him in his ongoing inquiries were two larger-than-life amateur criminologists, Lester Hodges and the enigmatically named Dr Fong. One other redeeming feature of this quirky programme was that Harry's next door neighbour was the gorgeous actress, Farrah Fawcett, the woman who later married the Bionic Man.

A few years after Scott had told me the myth of the Devonshire Harry O, we were playing Trivial Pursuit at my Nan's house. Scott shook the dice and landed on Entertainment. Then, somebody cleared their throat and read out this question: 'What profession does Harry O have?' to which Scott replied 'he's a tramp and he lives in Bradley Woods.' As you can imagine, that was not the answer on the card.

Alexandra the Great

THE Alexandra cinema stands almost directly in the middle of Newton Abbot. It is an old building which has been the centre of local entertainment for many years. Originally built as part of new market buildings in 1871, the buildings consisted of a pannier market, which included fish and vegetable markets, a new Corn Exchange and a public hall. This public hall was known as the Alexandra Hall and, in the early days, was used for concerts, lectures, even a skating rink. After a few years it was converted into a theatre with a stage being fitted and seating for 500 people. The first play ever staged in the Alexandra Theatre was *The Importance of Being Earnest*, which was performed in 1920 by the Newton Abbot Repertory Company. Later, it was converted into a cinema. One thing that I can vouch for is that there has always been drama at the Alex.

When I was a boy, the Alex was impressive and the inside had a beautiful Victorian splendour. There was a Gothic atmosphere seeping out of the walls. In those days, it had a circle upstairs, which is now a second screen. We always used to go up into the circle, and look down on the poor plebs in the stalls below. The main type of films that I can remember going to see as a child were Hollywood blockbusters like *Raiders of the Lost*

ABOVE: The Alex in about 1975. I've spent many happy hours in there watching men with white teeth fight men with black moustaches. BELOW: The Alex being refurbished in the 1970s. Note the filigree work on the balcony. Photos reproduced courtesy of Newton Abbot Museum.

Ark and *Star Wars*. The latter was a revelation. It had special effects which had not been seen before and when you're young, flashy stunts and effects can easily make up for any dire plot or story line. My friends and me collected *Star Wars* memorabilia until it filled our bedrooms. It was great. I can remember clutching on to my pocket money knowing that I was going to spend it on *Star Wars* stuff.

Sir Alex Guinness as Obi-Wan Kenobi was available in plastic form, but there were also an overabundance of plastic bit-part actors and actresses.

Another film which sticks in my mind is *ET* I can remember the cinema being packed with adults and young children. I can also remember men and women of all ages weeping like scolded babies at the bit where ET 'dies'. There was a whale of a woman bawling her eyes out; she sounded like a pocket air raid siren. My brothers and me thought it was hysterically funny. *Superman* stands out too. Christopher Reeve played the split personality role of Clark Kent/Superman with only a pair of NHS glasses as his disguise. Again, the special effects were eye-poppingly good (although they seem rather shabby when I look back on them now). It seems amazing to me that Christopher Reeve is now spinally injured and has a higher-level break than me (he has to breathe with the aid of a ventilator). Just goes to prove that disability can affect anybody.

The Alex became a different place when I was 17. I went there to watch films, but I would also socialise. Of course, booze was getting interesting, but the old habit of going to the Alex was still in me. Horror movies were great; a lot of schlock horror stuff came out in the mid-Eighties as did a great deal of National Lampoon's style comedies. Me and my friends would practically takeover the upper floor of the Alex and change it into a non-lethal battlefield. Popcorn made good ammunition but peanuts were better or even, specially brought in for the occasion, the mighty grape. Firing peanuts and empty drink cartons on to unsuspecting bald heads in the stalls was great fun. Sometimes I think these fights were due to the fact that some of the horror movies were quite frightening. *Nightmare On Elm Street* was particularly memorable to me. Wes Craven's first real horror flick gave you those neon flashing, rollercoaster thrills that made your Nan say 'it would've never happened in my day.' The most frightening part of that movie, for me, was when Freddie Kruger jumped out from behind a tree and I got hit on the back of the head with a grape.

I still go to the movies but I don't go to the Alex as often as I once did. The access has always been easy because there are no steps or thresholds. However, a few years ago, the owners decided to make the circle into an additional screen. So, I can only see half of the movies that come into the Alex because some are only shown on the upper screen. It's a real pain and to top it all, it has tarnished some of the Alex's internal good looks.

As well as movies, the Alex has a fine tradition in amateur dramatics. The Newton Abbot Amateur Dramatic Society has put on a variety of excellent productions over the years. My best friend Matthew (who is unfortunately no longer with us) used to appear in most of the productions especially in the last 10 years or so. Matthew enjoyed musicals although he used to admit that he was best suited to playing comedy roles, especially in pantomimes. He played the Dame, Simple Simon, Motel the Taylor in *Fiddler on the Roof*, the male lead in *Cabaret*, many other smaller parts and, probably his best role, Fagin in *Oliver*. Although, Matt used to take his acting quite seriously, Ialways remember the comedy parts and especially the blunders and cock-ups. During a performance of one of the pantomimes, a magic tree was supposed to snatch items which were being passed between two of the comedy characters. The magic tree was actually one of the members of the cast in a dodgy tree costume, which was stiff and seemed difficult to move about in. It was going well, and the sketch went off without a hitch, but as the magic tree shuffled into the background, the unfortunate inhabitant lost her footing and tumbled headlong into the scenery. The tree, now being in the horizontal position, was unable to move, so, to the sound of hysterical laughter from the audience, it was pulled off set by two-stage hands with its 'roots', or in this case welly-booted feet, kicking behind.

Another problem with pantomimes is that quite a few of the cast are cross-dressers. The dame is a man dressed as a woman, and the principal boy is a woman dressed as a man. This simple concept which is ingrained in British theatre is not so easy to understand if you are a child. Shouts of 'but that lady looks like a man' and 'why are those two girls holding hands?' are commonplace.

In a production of *Aladdin*, a possibly inebriated Abanazar made quite a few mistakes, the worst of which was when he eventually stole the magic lamp from Aladdin. He grasped the lamphungrily and shouted at the top of his voice 'ha ha ha! Now I *am* Aladdin!... Oh no I'm not!' which nearly made me and my dad have a coronary.

However, the funniest cock-up of them all was in the semi-serious musical *Fiddler On The Roof*. The scene in question is when Motel the Taylor is due to be wed to Tzeitel who is the daughter of Tevye (the main character, you know the one that was played in the film by Topol). As thecelebrations for the engagement are going

Sue, Matt and me in a snap taken at arms' length by Matt. He died within six months of this picture being taken.

ahead, one of the characters meets three drunken Russian soldiers coming back from the pub. He asks them'what are you celebrating?' to which one of the soldiers replied, in the broadest Devonshire accent I have ever heard, 'Tevyer's daughters getting married.' Well, my brother, Sue and me nearly died with laughing; tears were rolling down our cheeks. It wasn't the phrase that made us laugh, it was that the Russian soldier in question appeared to be from the Tavistock side of St Petersburg. The laughter was so loud that Matthew heard it backstage.

I'm worried about the Alex's future. I would like to see it restored to its original glory, but in the era of the multiplex cinema, small quaint theatres and cinemas are dying out. I want it to survive for selfish reasons; I have so many wonderful memories from there that I relive them every time I go back. So, the next time you're in Newton Abbot, you could check out the Alexandra Cinema. Don't expect to be blown away, it's not like it used to be. You could even try going to see the panto. If you do, then I'll see you there.

Dartmoor

WHEN I was a child everything was wonderful and somehow appeared important. The world seems made for children, and each experience is exciting and different. Being an adult only has one advantage as far as children can see; adults make the rules.

Children think that the type of issues which adults find interesting, and spend all their time dealing with, are superfluous and boring. As a child, it seemed as if adults only dealt with bizarre and tedious subjects that were uninteresting and bland. Whenever an adult opens his or her mouth, kids just want to yawn and fall asleep. It seems that adults have their priorities mixed up. They drone on and on about a weird thing called politics, which doesn't make any sense at all. The only issue that adults talk about which does seem important to children is the environment. Children are better at enjoying nature. They can splash in streams, climb trees, pretend they are Robin Hood and generally have a good time.

Since the 1960s, children have grown up watching that marvellous staple of British television, *Blue Peter*. The show where unusual quiffs and Arran jumpers come out for all to see. It is generally presented by three people who fall into the following categories: 1) the short adventurous male presenter who is sometimes forced to throw himself off cliffs, 2) the tall unadventurous male presenter who milks cows, wears unusual sweaters and spends a lot of time on his hair, and 3) the attractive female presenter who makes things out of washing-up liquid bottles, whom your dad quite fancies. *Blue Peter* shows you what children really think is important. When the subject of the environment comes up, they go the whole hog. Recycling, car-boot sales, fundraisers, running marathons, farmyard activities and so on. The writers of *Blue Peter* know that the children who watch the show want to grow up to be vets, ecologists, naturalists and people who work outdoors.

I can remember when I became an adult, other things jostled forward and started pushing my childhood standards out of the way. I was expected to worry about the things that adults consider important. Suddenly, I was expected to worry about politics. I began to worry about sex. I began to worry about cars, fridge-freezers, football teams, dishwashers, bank statements, electricity bills, potholes in the main road, pornography, aspidistras, endowment policies, stubborn milk cartons, vegetables, policemen, insurance, brassieres, dog poo, Xerox machines, floppy drives, bran, alcohol, cigarettes, dehumidifiers, money and so on. Suddenly, the environment was no longer as important as it had always seemed. Short term hedonism was the order of the day. Everything that I was told not to do, I did. A great deal of alcohol passed my tonsils in those days, and many sadly-missed brain cells died. In today's trashy throwaway world, many adults have forgotten that the environment was once so central to them. We grow up too soon.

When I was a child, one place of wonder was Dartmoor, the largest area of unenclosed land in the South. It seemed so big and inspiring, an adventurous place; there always seemed to be a chance that you might come across a pixie or elf just around the corner, hiding behind the impressive boulders. As a kid, my family was not into hiking and orienteering, we were just a Sunday picnic family. We would go to Haytor, Saddle Tor, Rippon Tor, Bonehill Rocks and Hound Tor. Amid the beautiful stones, me and my brothers might find a corpse of a dead crow or semi-rancid clods of wool. These type of things were excitingly real and showed us nature in its life and death glories. Humdrum everyday life doesn't seem as in-your-face as nature's gladiatorial struggles. In nature, death is a real and solid threat. It was the first time that I realised that death was not just something that happened to your elderly relatives and your guinea pigs, it was a natural event that happened all the time. I can remember seeing the corpse of a sheep with its eyeball glistening like a wet ball-bearing in its dead socket. I wanted to poke it with my little finger. I can feel the dread and excitement in my chest thinking about it now.

Yes, Dartmoor offered many treasures. Picking up a piece of granite was like finding a gold nugget. I would pick off bits of quartz and mica with my nails, and marvel at the shining pieces clinging to my fingertips. I would often pick up a stone and throw it as hard as I could into the deep bushes of gorse and heather, thinking that nobody else would ever touch it again from now until the end of time. Wilderness is a word which is seldom

My family walking on Dartmoor in the 1980s. The five people in the foreground are, from left, Mum, Steve, cousins Kate and Scott and my Aunty Janet. I'm in the far distance with Uncle Pete. The dog, Lucky, belonged to Aunty Jan.

used today, but Dartmoor is as close to wilderness as a West Country child will ever get.

Dartmoor today is a little bit alien to me. I still love it but, because I'm in a wheelchair, I can't experience it in the same way that I once did. A wheelchair is not the greatest all-terrain vehicle. I get stuck in ruts and bogged down in porridge-thick pathways. The small stones that I used to love have become giant obelisks which pound against my rickety wheels. I experience Dartmoor at arm's length. It is not a user-friendly place for me any more and I hate that. Even considering these facts, it still does mean a lot to me. It is a very special place.

A couple of months ago, I was travelling in my van from Newton Abbot to Kingsteignton, when I saw a man, his wife and their son, speeding ahead of us in a convertible sports car. I wasn't really paying much attention, but my eyes were fixed on the car in my half-awake state. Suddenly, I saw him throw a piece of rubbish over his wife's lap and out past the passenger side of the car into the hedge.

'My God!' I thought to myself, 'I can't believe he's just done that.'

I imagined pulling the man to one side and giving him a damn good talking to.

'What do you think you're doing, throwing crap out of your car?' I'd say.

'Have you any idea what this road would be like if everybody did that? I can tell you what it would be like, it would be knee-high in this type of shite!' (I was waving the piece of rubbish vigorously in my right hand by now).

'Oh, don't have a baby, man!' he would reply.

'It's only small, and I couldn't be arsed to take it home.'

'But, hang on! What type of influence do you think doing that has on your kid?' I would quickly retort.

'Are you serious?' he would ask. 'If you honestly think that what I've just done means I'm in the wrong, then I think you'd better roll up your sleeves and...'

It was at this point that I saw his son toss an identical piece of rubbish into the hedge.

ROUGH STUFF

A professor on my TV,
talked about the countryside
and spat out
so many half-truths
that they fell around his feet
like dead sparrows.

He said
'God's gift to *everyone* is the relief
of walking through the hills and woods.'
Then he squealed
'I am tired of marching on tarmac,'
and he headed for the rough stuff.

I say
dig out a trench
and place a thin sliver of hardness
through the wilderness,
then I could talk to him calmly,
without me
biting off his head.

Love and Death

WHAT exactly is love? John Lennon said that love is all you need, and a lot of people would agree with that, although today many people think that a big fat wallet helps – look at Lennon. For most of us, love is the big quest in life; our Holy Grail. I don't think that you can actually define or explain what love is unless you have experienced it firsthand.

Attraction between people is a mixture of hormones and mental compatibility. When you see somebody you are attracted to for the first time, you see them with your heart and your groin. Only later, when you get to know them, can you see if you mentally click. When you're young, the mental part doesn't seem to matter as much. Anyway, as a teenager, it's hard enough to concentrate on anything with all those hormones flying around inside your body. I can remember that even seeing a girl that I fancied, from anywhere within a 400 yard radius, would make my head turn somersaults. Me and my friends Matt and Ed would do anything to get a prime seat at the senior girls' 100 metres race at the school sports day. Phew! I'm sweating just thinking about it.

It's when you leave school that big relationships tend to happen. In South Devon, there are only a few options available to find your perfect partner.

Everybody has tried to pick people up in pubs at one time or other. It happens here as well but most people tend to go out in a group, so unless you're being introduced to your friends' friends, this can be a bit of a cul-de-sac. Nightclubs however are good hunting grounds. In big cities like London, the choice of nightclubs must be confusing and overwhelming but in this part of the world the choice is more limited. My local nightclubs have had some interesting nicknames over the years. When I was a student in Plymouth, one popular nightclub with a dodgy reputation was called *The Warehouse* but was known to many drinkers as The Whorehouse. Another amusingly nicknamed establishment was the so-called night club, *The Grasshopper* (which was situated in Ashburton). It was known locally as the Arse-Groper. Newton Abbot is much more upmarket. Well, when I say that I'm actually lying. Our local nightclub is *Rafters* and its nickname is Shafters, for obvious reasons. It is an unusual neon-tinted smoke-infested melting pot of a place, where you can practically scrape the testosterone off the walls. Sexual magnetism is the currency here and picking up a potential soulmate is unlikely. This is because only youngsters really go there and a good time is all they are looking for. Of course, everybody that goes to *Rafters* isn't young, there is also another category; the old and desperate.

My friend Paul, who also is a wheelchair user, goes there for the booze and an occasional stolen snog. He makes a special effort to go there on Foam Party Night to give his wheelchair what he calls 'a good wash.'

Another possibility in South Devon for romantic shenanigans is the club scene. No, not club as in some sort of rave thing, I mean the social clubs like the British Legion and the working-men's type clubs. Kingsteignton has a British Legion and our local social club, the *Oakford*, where Sue and some of my friends play for that great skittles team, The Dickie Bird's. We were introduced to skittles by our beer-loving, PhD-winning friend Chopper (real name Pete). Finding the love of your life at a skittles match is unlikely and you would have to be desperate to try it. Skittles is generally played by old men and women, by people who like beer, and by the occasional person who your mum probably wouldn't like. Anyway, most of them have some type of repetitive strain injury from bowling those rubber balls and from constantly picking up skittles so they might not be that good in the bedroom department. At a social club, you could go for somebody who likes playing darts, but these tend to be fat men fond of their beer, so unless you like that type of person you are probably barking up the wrong tree. I suppose you could go to support a local football club but if you're on your own and looking for love, it would probably be another dead end.

I noticed the other day that my local newspaper, *The Herald Express*, runs a personals column, but I don't think that this would have that good a success rate. From studying the notices, you can see that when a man first places an advert in the column, he starts with something like:

'Man aged 33 seeks buxom professional lady aged 18 to 24 with own house and GSOH. Non-smoker - no time-wasters please.'

But after weeks or months of failure the advert slowly begins to sound a bit desperate; along the lines of :

'Man aged 33 seeks woman with own teeth, aged 18 plus.'

Yes, love is hard to find. We all set out in life hoping to have that ideal relationship, the type that Romeo and Juliet had (although without the dire consequences) or the type that Kermit and Miss Piggy have (although without the excessive beatings).

Apart from the members of my family, I have loved two people. My partner Sue is the love of my life. We met in the sixth form and I fancied her from the outset. After getting to know her a little, I realised that we were very compatible and into the same type of things. We liked similar types of rock music and both of us were heavily into science-fiction and fantasy novels. For the first year or so, we just hung out together; listened to music, went on long walks in the countryside, went to parties and generally had a good time. It wasn't until our second year at sixth form that we became an item. After my accident, our relationship changed from easy second nature to hard graft. The type of life-changing incident that happened to the both of us would test the most sturdy of relationships. Ask yourself this question, could your relationship survive such a lightning bolt? Sue has made my life bearable with her love, support and commitment. Whatever the future holds for us, one thing I know for sure is that I'll always love her and I owe her more than I can ever say.

The second person that I have loved, and still love, was my best friend Matthew. We had known each other since we were toddlers and we grew up together. Matthew had mesmeric charisma, a creative wit and, when he wanted to call upon them, a copious repertoire of insults. He always had at his fingertips, a plethora of one-liners and classic put-downs that all of us wish that we could have said. He loved musicals, drama and amateur dramatics more than anything and he was the single most talented person I have ever known with a fantastic stage presence (especially when playing comedy roles) and a beautiful lilting voice.

He helped Sue and me through the best and worst times, and did the best Dracula impression in England. He died on Christmas Day 2000 from a debilitating disease called amyloidosis. This attacks every major organ in your body, depositing massive amounts of protein and basically, making you rot from the inside out. Every medical intervention failed but he never lost his dignity and his strength. He used to say that I was an inspiration to him and he never gave up fighting because of this fact. All that I can say is, I am not worthy of his adulation and that I miss him every single day.

Hang on a minute! Of course, the Three Musketeers! I used to think of me, Matt and our mate Ed as the Three Musketeers. Athos (that's me, the older, more physical one), Aramis (Matt, the foppish flamboyant one) and Porthos (Ed, the large beer-swilling food connoisseur). I've known my friend Ed since primary school and he is a great liver of life. He always has a smile on his face, is always ready for a challenge and has been a great source of support for me and Sue. What I'm getting at is I love my mate Ed as well (although I do not find him physically attractive, even if he does look good in a dress).

Thinking about Matt brings me to the subject of death. I have often thought about what it would be like to die, and what I would like my last words to be. I suppose that the majority of us would like to say something significant the very moment before we die. Something like 'you know Maude, I've always hated cheese,' or 'I've hidden the money under the floorboards.' A recent survey said that *My Way* was one of the most popular funeral tunes. I reckon that 'I did it my way,' would be right up there as popular last words. However, many people die without saying anything significant. It's often something like 'I'd like a cup of tea,' 'my back's giving me gyp,' or, even more

The Three Musketeers looking particularly stupid in about 1985. From left, there's Ed (looking like a cross between Ian Botham and a Dutch pimp), me (looking like a rent boy), and Matt (looking like he fancies the photographer).

likely, 'argggh.' Death in Devon is a sombre affair. It is a traditionally conservative area and even the most radical people are Liberal Democrats. This means that any unusual funeral arrangements are just that, unusual. I must say though that Devon funeral food tends to be excellent; it's one of those events that you are practically guaranteed to have a good feed. I once read in the local paper about a couple of elderly people who hardly bought any of their own food. They supplemented their diet by going to funerals and getting superb meals into the bargain. If they were ever interrogated by the family they would just say 'oh, we're friends of John,' which would get them past most people. It just goes to show that funerals can leave you feeling depressed but they can also leave you feeling totally stuffed.

When I die I'd like to be remembered by my friends and family recalling all the fun and good times we shared. Just sprinkle my ashes in Fairwater Leat in Kingsteignton and move on. After all, I'm only a Numpty.

I'd like my funeral to be an interesting event, with a free bar and a disco afterwards; I reckon everybody would appreciate that. At the actual funeral, I would love to have *Jerusalem* and *Lord of the Dance* as hymns, and, as the songs played as people left, I would choose *Slow Marching Band* by Jethro Tull (a lovely ballad), *Voodoo Chile* by

Jimi Hendrix and I feel it would be a missed opportunity if I did not have *Living in a Box* by Living in a Box.

Hopefully, the afterlife will be nice. Even if there isn't any afterlife as such, there will be a lovely silence (at least I won't be pained by my tinnitus which I have to suffer because of going to too many heavy rock concerts in my youth). I reckon though that death is a blessing; after all there are only so many times you can watch *Goldfinger* or repeats of Morecambe and Wise Christmas specials. One thing I know for sure is that it will be nice to taste my Nan Yeo's sausage rolls again.

Who's a Numpty Now?

BEFORE we finish, I'd better give you a quick lesson in how to use the word 'numpty'. I use it quite a lot. It is an excellent and superbly descriptive term, just a little bit stronger than 'buffoon' and not as rude as 'twat'.

Numpty is not often used as a direct insult to disabled people. When referring to disabled people, more often than not 'numpty' has the word 'bus' attached. When you call someone a numpty you should do so in a joking, non-serious way. Some examples of how to use it properly are; when referring to an old person making an unusual move in a car; when watching somebody hit their head on a Mind your Head sign; when a close friend does something dangerous 'for a laugh', or when your son deliberately hurts himself to see how much it would hurt. All of these people can be numpties.

There is another category of people, whom I meet often, who should not be confused with numpties. I call them Strange People. I have a lot of dealings with Strange People and have met them on many different occasions. They do not really warrant the use of the word 'weirdo' because they're just not quite weird enough. These people are almost completely normal but they are just the wrong side of the normality barrier; they are normal with a twist of bonkers. George Wakeham was a fine example of a Strange Person. He was a local character who lived in Chudleigh but often frequented the watering holes of Kingsteignton. As a child, I can remember him very well. He could be frequently seen at *The Dewdrop Inn* where the local football team, Kingsteignton Athletic, would change before and after matches. Because my dad was a keen local footballer, me and my brothers sometimes went to the pub to meet him, and George always seemed to be there. He was like a scary ogre to me. He was physically huge and wore false teeth that flew out at any given occasion. One of his favourite games was charades. He only ever had one mime, the answer to which was the word 'trophy' which was incidentally his favourite type of beer.

When George had had enough to drink he would lie in the middle of Kingsteignton High Street tapping passing motor cars with his walking stick. Almost as soon as he had started this, the police would pick him up in a panda car and take him home. The last time I saw him he was leading the Kingsteignton majorettes down the road twirling his walking stick in the air. George died quite a while ago leaving an unexpectedly large amount of money.

A wheelchair user completely challenges a Strange Person's view of the world. It is not that they do not understand what a wheelchair user is, but they recognise wheelchair users as being somehow different. Strange People that I generally meet in the street come in a variety of different categories. The first is people who are totally dumbstruck by me. They just stand there, in awe, like they have just seen Gandhi riding past them on a bicycle wearing nothing but a T-shirt with 'I love Satan' written on the back. They cannot even speak. They stand there like statues until I roll out of sight.

Another category is The Kissers. In other words, people who have an overwhelming desire to kiss me. Once, when I was in Cheltenham, an old tramp wearing denim and reeking of cider tried to kiss me, smack on the lips, for no apparent reason. There is a young woman who lives in Newton Abbot who often tries to kiss me given the opportunity. I met her in *The Bell Inn* (my local from Kingsteignton). As I positioned myself near a table with my friends, she beckoned my brother Steve over. Apparently, she whispered in his ear, 'is he all right?' to which my brother answered 'yes, he's fine.' She then said 'can I give him a little kiss?' to which my brother said 'no, you bloody well can't!'

Anyway, she wouldn't leave until she got a kiss. I saw her more recently in a local bookshop as I was paying for a book. She said to me 'oh, hello,'

and turning to the sales assistant said 'ain't he lovely?'
I said 'oh, shite!' and shouted to my carer: 'Don't ask! Just push fast now!'
We accelerated hard behind the children's video section. After I quickly explained what was happening, we sped out of the shop, quicker than Linford Christie on prune juice, with the young woman puckering up behind me.

The next category, is the Unsubtle Starer, people who just *have* to take a look at me, but think that I don't know they're doing it. I was in a pub in Paignton once with Matt and Sue. Matt was quickly polishing off a disgustingly greasy beef jacket potato, when the man sitting in the cubicle in front of me suddenly popped his head up over the top of the partition. Then he slowly popped his head out of the side of the partition, at the horizontal about three feet off the floor, which caused Sue to laugh out loud. He popped his head out again and again. I can still see him now; he is etched in my mind, looking like a cross between Basil Fawlty and Beaker from *The Muppets*.

Yet another category is the people who comment about me out loud without knowing they are doing it. You might say that these people get their mouths going before their brains are in gear. A middle-aged woman I often meet in Newton Abbot at an excellent vegetarian cafe, falls into this category quite neatly. The first time I saw her, I was happily drinking my coffee when she shouted out for no apparent reason: 'What a bunch of bloody jokers!'

'Christ,' I thought to myself, 'I hope that she doesn't see me.' But of course she had. I took a bite of my teacake. She saw this and said: 'Oh, bugger! He can't even feed himself! Oh my God!'

My Strange Person alarm went off. I tried not to make eye contact, and explained to my carer that we had better leave as quickly as possible. As we pushed out of the exit, I heard her say: 'I can walk, me!'

Before I discuss my favourite category, here are some other examples; people who salute me, tramps who go out of their way to open a door for me, elderly gentleman who feel that they can push me uphill much more easily than my strapping 24-year-old carer, and old women who want to give me their sandwiches.

Now I come to my favourite category of Strange Person: The Fallers. These are people that have to, and I mean really have to, take a surreptitious glance at me without me seeing, and, because of their attempts to be subtle, they trip up and fall flat on their arses. I like this category because, in a devilish way, I love to see people hurt themselves. Of course, I don't want them to *really* hurt themselves, just enough for it to sting a bit. My first experience of this was when I was newly injured. A woman in Plymouth fell flat on her hands because she just *had* to take a look at me. She turned her head around to look, and caught her toe on a kerb and went down like a redwood tree in lumberjack country.

More recently, when I was on holiday in Cornwall, I was sat on the cliffs at Treyarnon Bay in full sun, when a young man appeared out of nowhere. I am susceptible to the sun and turn red quite easily, so I was kitted up with a baseball cap and, for extra protection, I was wearing as a type of headscarf, a pair of Omani underpants, which are not really pants, just large cotton handkerchief-like cloths. This pair of Omani underpants happen to be pink. So, picture the scene, I was sat there, a man in a wheelchair, wearing a baseball cap, and a pink scarf.

The young man was, I believe, slightly taken aback by this, had to have a quick glance at this disabled, possibly homosexual sun worshipper, and, as he took a sneaky look, he promptly stuck his foot down a hole and fell over on to a gravel path. I inwardly chuckled to myself, and then I realised that this guy had only missed falling off the cliff by about two feet! At least as well as being slightly strange this lad was also lucky.

A worrying thought came to me the other day. I realised that one person's concept of 'strange' is different to everybody else's. We believe that bank managers, accountants, postman, farmers, solicitors, receptionists, policemen and teachers are normal, but doesn't their normality make them even stranger than your average Strange Person. Are you normal if you're a white, clean-shaven accountant with a wife, two kids, a labrador, Ford Escort, with a yucca plant in the downstairs hall and a Toilet Duck in the upstairs lav? Perhaps the Strange People in the world (and there seem to be a hell of a lot of them) are in fact the only normal people among us. Perhaps it's everybody else that's strange.

That reminds me of a true story. One of my ex-carers, called Jim, was once required by his care agency to work at a psychiatric unit. He was introduced to a young man that required one-on-one care.

'Hello, my name's Jim,' he said.

'Pleased to meet you,' said the young man.

There was a slight pause.

'Just because I'm in here, doesn't mean I'm crazy you know,' said the young man abruptly.

'Oh, I know that,' replied Jim, 'You can be in here and be as normal as the next man.'

The young man smiled smugly.

'Yes,' he said, 'I've got a certificate from the doctor which proves it.'

He dived into a small chest of drawers and

produced a large piece of paper. 'There,' he said handing the paper to Jim.

Jim looked at the piece of paper, and in the middle of it in large red letters was printed the word, SANE.

'Oh yes, that proves it then,' said Jim hoping to appease his patient.

There was another, longer pause while both parties smiled nervously. Jim twiddled his thumbs while the patient bounced up and down lightly on his bed.

Suddenly, the silence was broken.

'Could I see *your* certificate now please?' asked the young man.

Wile E. Coyote

IF you asked most people they would probably say that if they were totally paralysed from the neck down, as I am, they would consider committing suicide.

In my worst bouts of depression, I fantasise about ending my life and occasionally dream about it, but I decide, in my head, that it would be no 'cry for help', no eight paracetamols and a Lemsip. I would make sure. I see myself jumping off the town centre multi-storey car park in Torquay. Then I think about more definite methods. So I envisage jumping off the car park's top floor, but with a stick of dynamite in each pocket, which I light on the way down, blowing off both my legs before I get run over by a truck full of bricks. I see myself lying on my back in a dingy in the middle of Plymouth harbour, shooting myself in the mouth with a double-barrelled shotgun, creating a hole in a boat so that I sink to the bottom and get eaten by bottom feeding flat fish. I imagine crouching in a cornfield, drinking a bottle of sulphuric acid, just before I get run over by a combine harvester driven by Daffy Duck.

That's the strange thing, I seem to be part of some type of cartoon-like suicide fantasy, almost like a *Roadrunner* cartoon, but without Roadrunner. The only character in this dream is me, Wile E. Coyote, committing suicide in more and more bizarre ways. Being run over by a train, carrying Acme glue. Being pounded into the deck by a giant rock fired from a hydraulic catapult. Being crushed by an anvil, which has been covered in tacks, after I've eaten a plate full of poisoned birdseed. It's just so bizarre.

Although you may smile, I'm deadly serious in my fantasies. When I imagine killing myself, I really, *really* want to be fucking dead.

And that is the part that galls me; thinking in a cartoon-like way almost turns my suicide fantasies into trivia. It is as if my dreams are mocking me, forcing me to think of death in unusual ways, showing me that my fantasising is paper-thin, unrealistic and deluded. I am like a hamster on a wheel, going over the same old ground, in a never-ending spiral of depression. To make it worse, I relate to the cartoon characters who, no matter what happens to them, keep on living. They bounce back to be pulverised, mashed and blown up again and again without ever dying, and I persevere in a similar way, carrying on no matter what setbacks I encounter, but still ultimately wanting to be dead.

However, it is this last fact which, when I think about it, fills me with hope. I am resilient, I am tough, and I do survive. I am a disabled person and, although sometimes I hate my disability, I carry on in the way that the majority of disabled people do, with dignity and determination. It is when I am at my lowest that I often realise I do not want to die, I do not want to commit suicide, I am a worthwhile, important and optimistic person who does have a quality of life that many people would envy. I hope that I never forget that.

We are all caricatures, we are all twisted parodies. You never really thought about it but, at times, Tony Blair *is* Peter Perfect, Michael Jackson *is* Mickey Mouse, George Bush *is* a strange cross between Yosemite Sam and Mister Magoo. And as for me, well... I am Wile E. Coyote.

End Thoughts

THE future always arrives unexpectedly. Today's new technology is amazing. We have DVD players that bring cinema-style clarity to your TV, and mobile phones where your average Star Trek fan can pretend to be James T. Kirk or Seven of Nine (depending on whether you like toupees or push-up bras).

New technology affects me directly. Not only by allowing me to use a computer, which I do through a mouse headset and through my voice, but also through my Possum. This does not mean that I have a nocturnal, arboreal Australian marsupial running about my house, but that I have an environmental control system which allows me to take control of the television, the video, and various household electrical items. Technological advances have allowed me to gain a degree of independence which I could never have had only a few years ago.

The future will also bring many medical break-throughs. As far as I'm concerned, innovations in treating spinal injury are not so certain. Since Christopher Reeve broke his neck, there has been a lot of publicity about spinally injured people especially as he is adamant that he will walk again. If anybody can do it, he can because he has the backing of so many people. A medical step forward may come through the use of stem cells, which is a highly exciting area of research. Also, due to gene laws in America, any breakthrough may occur here in the UK.

I regard a cure for the spinally injured in the same way as I regard supporting Torquay United. With Torquay, I always hope every season that they will win the league but I know it's unlikely. However, its uncertainty doesn't stop me from hoping that it will happen, and that's the same way that I view any cure. Many people have said that hoping for a cure is encouraging false hope and therefore spinally injured people will not get on with their lives. I think that is shite. People invariably do get on with their lives and, after all, hope is important. I think it is better to be an optimist than a pessimist and anyway, it just might happen.

When I think about what the future holds for me, my mind becomes full of things that I hope will happen. They are: that Torquay United will improve, that I stay fit and healthy, that I enjoy my life, that I spend it with Sue, that a cure for spinal injuries is found, that I become a successful author.

As the Numpty Bus slows to a halt, I can tell you where to find the common Numpty, but I think you already know the answer. Like a virus, the effect of the Numpty is widespread. It only takes a moment of speculation to realise that you're a Numpty and everybody else seems to be one as well. We are not Numpties all of the time but most of us are most of the time. The realisation came to me one day that Numpties are everywhere. They are the tramp picking up a dog-end, the checkout girl at a supermarket, the driver cutting me up, boxers, free climbers, stuntmen and so on. Not only are these people Numpties but you begin to think that maybe your brother, your sister, your mum and your dad are as well. There comes a stark realisation that Numpties have wangled their way into history, fame and politics. Kennedy was a Numpty, Churchill was a Numpty, Hitler was a *big* Numpty. I am a Numpty and so are you. After all, you're the one who is reading this book. Chances are that you decided to read this book when you could have been doing something more interesting and invigorating. You could have been having sex, eating a rare steak, having a hot bath, walking in the woods, asking out that girl (or boy) that you never had the guts to ask out. You could even have been writing your own book or doing that thing that you always wished you had the time to do. And you decided to read *this* book. You could have been reading the *Bible* or the *Koran*. You could have been reading *Hamlet* or *King Lear*. You could have been reading a book by D.H. Lawrence, Salman Rushdie, Sir Walter Scott,

H.G. Wells, Peter Carey or some poetry by Ted Hughes or Spike Milligan.

But when I say these words, I'm not being abusive or knocking you in any way; being a Numpty is what makes us all human. It is our fallibility that allows us to learn, teaches us right from wrong and shows us that nobody is above being foolish from time to time. Let's face it, knowing that people such as world leaders can be fallible, can be Numpties, gives us a connection with them (sometimes our only connection).

Join the club. Join the human race. As you hold up this book, reading these words, you're holding up a mirror. Look deep into the page, my brothers and sisters, and read these words out loud: 'Thank God, I am a Numpty!'

WRITING POETRY

It's like fishing
with hands
in a muddy puddle.

Like juggling teapots
filled with lobsters.

Like mixing up
breakneck
and slumber
in a meaningless jumble,
with more or less passion
than a kiss,
with the qualities
of ephemera,
with the ambition
to get to the end.

And when I finish,
I am spent
and only later
can I see
its head
or its tail
or whether it lies
on its side

which
it nearly
always
does.

ACKNOWLEDGEMENTS

Thanks to the following people and groups who have helped me bring this book into being:

All my family and Sue's family too for their tireless support. My good friends, Ed, Matt, Maria, and Chopper, who kept my mind full of inspiration.

Richard Harris for his information about our family's history and the old Kingsteignton photos.

All of my carers, past and present.

Newton Abbot Museum for providing many of the photographs of Newton Abbot.

For all at EQUATA – the first organisation to spot my work – especially to Linda Lawrence, Gary Goodwin and Penny Goater. My editor Sara Hudston. All those people whose time and effort have helped me in any way.

And special thanks to Sue whose love and support made it all possible.

As an extra piece though, I have to pay homage to the people who are like a group of alternative beat poets and raconteurs without even knowing it. Their storytelling abilities are second to none and have fed me with enough subject matter to sink a polystyrene whale.

Final thanks to an 'old bag' who shall remain nameless.

Martin Wildman

ABOUT THE AUTHOR

Martin Wildman was born in 1968 in South Devon. He is tetraplegic spinally injured wheelchair user who broke his neck in 1990 and has been writing poetry since 1996. He now focuses primarily on prose and writes with the use of an adapted computer. His study is crammed with a variety of books ranging from 20Th century poetry to science-fiction. He attended Knowles Hill Sixth Form, Newton Abbot in 1984 before embarking on a three year degree course in Accountancy at Plymouth University.

Martin's pieces have been published in small press magazines and his work has also appeared in exhibitions. One of his poems is displayed in the access lift at Bristol's Watershed Arts Centre.

SELECTED COMMISSIONS:

1999 *Art by Post* exhibition, appearing in various South West libraries.

2000 EQUATA's Poet in Residence (for one year), Exeter Phoenix Centre.

2000 *Animals! Animals!* exhibition, working with children with learning difficulties from Bidwell Brook school, Dartington, displayed at Dartington Hall.

2000 *Life Like Fiction* exhibition, focusing on lifts, with photographer Gary Goodwin, Exeter Phoenix Centre.

Agre Books is a small, independent publisher that specialises in non-fiction books about South West subjects. Based in Dorset, it covers the South West peninsula from Bristol and Bath down to the Isles of Scilly.

Agre takes its name from the legend of Actaeon and Diana as told in Ovid's Metamorphoses. Ovid names Actaeon's hounds and lists their attributes. 'The thicket-searcher Agre' was the hound with the keenest nose. Agre Books searches the thickets of its distinctly rural region to find interesting truths and intriguing stories.

Titles published include:

ISLOMANIA (£6.50) by Sara Hudston, with 21 photographs from the Gibson Archive on the Isles of Scilly. Islomania - an obsession with islands. Why are islands so captivating? Using the Isles of Scilly off Cornwall as its example, this book explores the phenomenon of islomania.

THE WHEAL OF HOPE (£9.99). Poems and notes by James Crowden, with 35 black and white pictures by Dorset photographer George Wright. The closure of South Crofty, the last working tin mine in Cornwall, marked the end of more than 3,000 years of history. This book pays tribute to the men, women and children whose lives shaped Cornwall's unique industrial landscape.

FOR LOVE OF WILLIAMINA (£6.99) by Ralph Rochester. Williamina Belsches' beauty captured the heart of the young Walter Scott. At the age of only 32 she contracted consumption and sought relief in the sea-breezes of Lympstone in Devon, then the haunt of many fashionable invalids. This romantic account gives an unsurpassed picture of East Devon society during late-Georgian times.

THE CORNISH PASTY (£4.99) by Stephen Hall. A complete history of the original hand-held fast food from medieval times to the present day. Includes recipes, folklore and old postcards.

SWITCH OFF THE LIGHT AND LET ME TRY ON YOUR DRESS (£9.99). Paintings and drawings by John Skinner with commentary by Sara Hudston. This limited edition chronicles Skinner's work in Dorset over the last decade, providing an unusual and thought-provoking insight into the creative process. With 21 full-colour reproductions.

A DORSET UPTOPIA by Judith Stinton (forthcoming for 2003). During the 1910s, the educational psychologist Homer Lane established an progressive community in a remote corner of Dorset. Using new material never before published, this book reveals a fascinating picture of one of the first practical experiments in progressive education.

To find out more about Agre you can write to Agre Books, Groom's Cottage, Nettlecombe, Bridport, Dorset, DT6 3SS or visit the website at www.agrebooks.co.uk

ABOUT THE PRINTING OF THIS BOOK
All Aboard the Numpty Bus was typeset by Agre Books in Monotype Imprint. The cover was designed by Stuart Brill at Senate Design and the book was printed and bound on 130gsm matt art paper by Short Run Press of Exeter.